Celebrations

Christmas

Jennifer Gillis

Raintree

www.raintreepublishers.co.uk
Visit our website to find out more information about **Raintree** books.

To order:
 Phone 44 (0) 1865 888112
Send a fax to 44 (0) 1865 314091
Visit the Raintree Bookshop at **www.raintreepublishers.co.uk** to browse our catalogue and order online.

First published in Great Britain by Raintree, Halley Court, Jordan Hill, Oxford OX2 8EJ, part of Harcourt Education.
Raintree is a registered trademark of Harcourt Education Ltd.

Editorial: Jennifer Gillis (HL-US) and Diyan Leake
Design: Sue Emerson (HL-US) and Michelle Lisseter
Picture Research: Amor Montes de Oca (HL-US) and Maria Joannou
Production: Lorraine Hicks

Originated by Dot Gradations
Printed and bound in China by South China Printing Company

ISBN 1 844 21520 2
07 06 05 04 03
10 9 8 7 6 5 4 3 2 1

British Library Cataloguing in Publication Data
Gillis, Jennifer
Christmas
394.2'663
A full catalogue record for this book is available from the British Library.

Acknowledgements
The publishers would like to thank the following for permission to reproduce photographs: Barrett & Mackay Photography Inc. pp. 11, 14; Bruce Coleman Inc./Bradley Olman pp. 4, 22, 23 (Christmas tree), 24, back cover (Christmas tree); Corbis pp. 12 (Chris Carroll), 15 (Becky Luigart-Stayner), 17 (Douglas Peebles), 18 (Douglas Peebles), 19 (David Katzenstein), 20, 21 (Steve Chenn), 23 (bow, wreath, Chris Carroll), back cover (biscuits, Becky Luigart-Stayner); Craig Mitchelldyer pp. 8, 9, 13, 23 (ornament); DDB Stock Photo p. 10 (Robin J. Dunitz); Jerome Longawa pp. 5, 23 (Jesus); PictureQuest p. 23 (Saint Nicholas, Florence Salter/Wood River Gallery); TRIP pp. 7 (H. Rogers), 16 (S. Grant)

Cover photograph of Christmas, reproduced with permission of Imagestate/First Light

Every effort has been made to contact copyright holders of any material reproduced in this book. Any omissions will be rectified in subsequent printings if notice is given to the publishers.

Some words are shown in bold, **like this.** You can find them in the glossary on page 23.

Contents

What is Christmas?

Christmas is a celebration.

It is a special time for many people.

Christmas is a special day for people who believe in **Jesus**.

They remember the day he was born.

When do people celebrate Christmas?

DECEMBER						
1	2	3	4	5	6	7
8	9	10	11	12	13	14
15	16	17	18	19	20	21
22	23	24	25	26	27	28
29	30	31				

Christmas Day is 25 December.

But Christmas time is more than one day.

People put up Christmas decorations early in December.

They go to Christmas parties and concerts all month.

What do people do at Christmas?

On Christmas Day, some people go to church.

They may spend the day with their families.

Some people sing Christmas songs called carols.

What are Christmas lights like?

Candles at Christmas make a pretty light.

There are candles inside churches.

There are lights on **Christmas trees**.

There are lights on houses and buildings.

What do Christmas decorations look like?

wreath

bow

There are green Christmas **wreaths** and **Christmas trees**.

There are red **bows** on the wreaths.

There are coloured Christmas tree lights and **ornaments**.

There are decorations in the shape of stars and snowflakes.

What food do people eat at Christmas?

Some people have a special dinner on Christmas Day.

They may cook a turkey or a ham.

Some people make special biscuits for Christmas.

The biscuits can be shaped like bells, stars or trees.

How do people dress at Christmas time?

In some places, it is very cold at Christmas time.

People in those places wear warm clothes.

In other places, it is very hot
at Christmas time.

People there dress to stay cool.

What stories do people tell at Christmas?

The Christmas story tells how **Jesus** was born.

Some children act out this story in a **nativity play**.

Some people read a famous poem on the night before Christmas.

The poem tells about a visit from **Saint Nicholas**.

Who gives presents at Christmas?

People give each other presents at Christmas time.

Some children make a list of the things they want.

There are presents under the **Christmas tree**.

Who puts them there?

Quiz

What are these Christmas things called?

Look for the answers on page 24.

?

?

?

Glossary

bow
way of tying ribbon in loops

Christmas tree
special tree decorated for Christmas

Jesus
the baby whose birth is celebrated
at Christmas

nativity play
play about the birth of Jesus

ornament
something pretty to put on a
Christmas tree

Saint Nicholas
Father Christmas, or the person who
brings presents at Christmas time

wreath
leaves or flowers made into a circle

Index

Answers to quiz on page 22

ornament

lights

presents

Titles in the Celebrations series include:

Hardback   1 844 21523 7

Hardback   1 844 21520 2

Hardback   1 844 21521 0

Hardback   1 844 21522 9

Find out about the other titles in this series on our website www.raintreepublishers.co.uk